GCSEs

A Parent's Guide

Charlotte Evans

GCSEs – A Parent's Guide is also available in accessible formats for people with any degree of visual impairment. The large print edition and e-book (with accessibility features enabled) are available from Need2Know. Please let us know if there are any special features you require and we will do our best to accommodate your needs.

First published in Great Britain in 2012 by
Need2Know
Remus House
Coltsfoot Drive
Peterborough
PE2 9BF
Telephone 01733 898103
Fax 01733 313524
www.need2knowbooks.co.uk

Contents

Introduction

For parents, the whole GCSE experience can be a bit of a shock. For perhaps the first time in your child's life, you are realising how very grown up they are becoming. You are also realising that you need to allow your child to start taking responsibility for themselves and their future. It's a daunting thing.

The purpose of this Need2Know guide, though, is to help you through that somewhat trying process of seeing your child starting to grow up. With the GCSE study programme, you can expect to see your child starting to think about their future.

Although it is one of several steps, the process of selecting GCSE subjects does involve some consideration about what your child wants to do for a career and where they want to go with their knowledge, skills and abilities.

GCSEs are also a time for children to start learning and demonstrating time management skills, independent study skills, and an overall higher level of thinking that sets them on the way to higher education or the like.

Although no book can offer all the answers for parents going through the GCSE process, this informative and practical book will help you address issues with the process of subject selection, time management through Years 10 and 11, questions about coursework, and exam preparation. It also offers some suggestions about how to handle the decidedly stressful period between the end of the exam period and results day.

Although there are a lot of books, websites and articles out there that explain what GCSEs are and why they are important, it is still difficult for Year 10 students, let alone their parents, to truly get a sense of what the GCSE exams are and what the experience of taking them will be.

This book concentrates on the parent – your role in helping your child approach and work through GCSEs. A key objective is to help you understand how you can best support your child through this experience and what steps you can take, as a parent, to ensure that your child has the best chance of success.

One of the biggest challenges for parents, and the reason why we have established our initial chapter as an overview, is the difficulty gauging what the GCSE experience is actually like.

If you grew up in the United Kingdom in the last several decades, you are probably not unfamiliar with GCSE exams, the stress they encourage, and why they are important. Your knowledge, however, is likely to be somewhat out of context and out of date. Unless you have already seen a child through the modern GCSE process, you probably don't have a clear reference point to determine what it is like to parent a child going through these exams or to experience the GCSEs as a parent.

It is difficult to gauge any experience when you have no real point of reference. New, inexperienced teachers and parents have something in common because they have to go back to their own memories of GCSEs, which may not be reflective of the typical experience for GCSE students today. The exams have changed over the years (not to put too fine a point on it, parents and teachers probably took GCSEs at least a decade ago, if not more). Parents approaching the GCSEs for the first time as parents are also probably going to have to rely on their recollection of their own GCSE experience. The one exception might be if the parent is also a teacher of GCSE-level students. However, even with this exception, we have another issue. Parents and teachers remembering past experiences or even extrapolating on more recent experiences (experiences of other children in the family, of students taught by the parent, etc.) still cannot accurately predict what the experience will be for each and every child. It's all part of this broader issue that you can't really determine one person's experience based on someone else's.

All you can really do is educate yourself to be aware of all of the possible issues that may arise, and take steps to prepare yourself and your child to handle them. In a nutshell, this education is what this book sets out to provide. To learn more about possible issues, though, in addition to reading this book, there are a few strategies you can undertake right off the bat. First, it's a safe bet to assume that many teachers have a reasonable amount of knowledge going through the GCSE process. Even though their experience and knowledge is not necessarily going to be absolutely applicable to your child, you can still go to your child's teachers to get some initial feedback and insight. Second, students who have just taken GCSE exams can also be a good source of information, of first-hand and recent accounts of issues such as workload, stress, academic challenges, time management strategies, and more. It may be a good idea, starting out, to have our child buddy up with someone who has recently completed the GCSE exams. In addition to giving you and your child some initial insight into the GCSE experience – a place to start – sitting down and talking to teachers and students with recent experience may help you begin to gauge potential problems and strengths that your child may be able to apply during the GCSE period.

In this book, there are several phases of the GCSE experience that we are going to consider.

First we are going to consider preparation. We will cover the build-up to the GCSE examinations. We will discuss the transition to secondary school and cover everything from the selection of schools at that point, right the way through to choosing GCSE subjects and other planning phases that relate to the two years of school that are devoted to the GCSE courses.

Next we will discuss the process of studying for GCSEs, covering both general study tips and specific revision periods, including tips on how you can help your child study and revise in preparation for their exams.

We will talk about ideas and strategies to help you help your child through the exam period with minimum stress and maximum efficiency. We will also cover exam techniques and stress management tools that you can teach your child, as well as tips on helping your child to stay healthy and relaxed during their exams.

Finally, we will also cover the post-GCSE period, including results day. To help you help your child use their GCSE results, we will also offer suggestions on what you need to encourage your child to think about and plan for after their exams, as they think about post-GCSE options and possible career choices.

Chapter One

GCSEs: An Overview

What are GCSEs?

GCSE stands for General Certificate of Secondary Education.

GCSEs are an academic qualification that are awarded in individual subjects and taught to students in secondary school (usually between the ages of 14 and 16) in England, Wales and Northern Island.

Why are they important?

In your child's school career, the GCSEs are just one of several forms of standardised assessments used by schools to gauge your child's ability in different subjects and skills areas relative to their peers. Standardised testing is all about comparing one individual's results against the results of the majority. What you will notice when you read more about how GCSEs are graded is that a percentile system is used and grades are adjusted based on where students score each year.

The importance of the GCSEs, though, is determined by their status as the first of two sets of exams that tend to have a very direct impact upon your child's educational and professional future. Next to A levels, GCSE results are what colleges and even some employers look at to determine whether your child is a suitable candidate for a particular position. Not only do GCSE results demonstrate your child's abilities in different areas; the subjects they study and excel at at GCSE also go some way to demonstrating your child's interests in different subjects, outlining their possible career paths.

'GCSEs are an academic qualification that are awarded in individual subjects and taught to students in secondary school (usually between the ages of 14 and 16) in England, Wales and Northern Island.'

More immediately, GCSE results may very well determine whether your child receives a place at their school or local community college to study for A level. They can also impact whether your child is likely to be accepted to study a particular subject at A level. Although it is rare that a school will refuse to allow someone to take a given subject at A level because of results at GCSE, if your child scores poorly in their GCSE exams for a subject that they want to study at A level, their teachers may advise against studying that same subject at A level. This is definitely something to keep in mind.

Because of the impact these exams have on everything from sixth form placement to A level choices, college options, and future careers, doing well at GCSE is very important.

What are International GCSEs (IGCSEs)?

International GCSEs are a particular style of GCSE examination that were previously only taken by students at independent schools.

These exams are similar to the GCSEs in England, Wales and Northern Ireland, and the so-called Standard Grade in Scotland or Junior Certificate in the Republic of Ireland.

The IGCSEs were developed by University of Cambridge International Examinations in 1988. Today, the University of Cambridge International Examinations offers IGCSEs in over 70 subjects, including 30 languages.

Today, however, Edexcel also offers its own version of the IGCSE, called Edexcel IGCSE.

Although they are not 'standard' forms of examination, the key thing you need to know about these exams is that they are often compared to the O level exams that modern GCSEs replaced. They are intended to be different from the standard GCSEs – more easily recognised as an international standard qualification.

If your child's school offers to prepare students for IGCSEs instead of GCSEs, it is important to sit down with the teacher or teachers who would be responsible for teaching your child to find out what the individual courses might entail. You should also talk with your child about the advantages and disadvantages of taking an IGCSE instead of a standard GCSE in whatever subject or subjects your child is considering.

Determining when your child will begin studying for GCSEs

Most schools begin teaching GCSE course material at the end of Year 9, once the Key Stage 3 examinations are out of the way. In Year 9, though, the focus of GCSE-level teaching is usually coursework and usually only in certain subject areas, such as English, maths and science (core subjects that your child will have to continue studying through GCSE anyway).

Should your child take GCSEs earlier or later?

There are certainly instances in which gifted or particularly capable students take GCSE courses and examinations early. There are also instances in which GCSE examination may be delayed to allow a child more time to learn to perform at an appropriate level.

Whether your child should take GCSEs earlier or later than usual (Year 10 to 11) is something that your child's teachers will be able to help you determine. If you feel your child may be capable of taking the exams early and succeeding, consider setting up an appointment with your child's teacher (or whoever else at your child's school is responsible for overseeing Years 10 and 11 or GCSE exams). If you feel your child might benefit from waiting any length of time before taking GCSE examinations, make an appointment to talk to their teacher about your concerns and communicate with your child to ascertain their opinion – ask them whether they feel ready, based on their understanding of what GCSEs involve.

'Most schools begin teaching GCSE course material at the end of Year 9, once the Key Stage 3 examinations are out of the way.'

What GCSE study involves

The particulars of GCSE study vary by course, and even then by exam board and school. Different exam boards set different requirements for GCSE and schools have the further option to pick between topics. For instance, in the study of history, there tends to be flexibility as to which period of history is studied at GCSE.

Generally speaking, GCSE courses are taught over two years from Year 10 to Year 11, and taken by students aged between 14 and 16.

Up to ten subjects are taken as GCSE-level subjects and the courses themselves involve assessment through coursework, final exams, and other assessments that may include teacher feedback and practical examinations (for example).

'Generally speaking, GCSE courses are taught over two years from Year 10 to Year 11, and taken by students aged between 14 and 16.'

Some recent changes to GCSES – most notably to the so-called core subjects of English, ICT and maths – have increased the amount of 'controlled assessment' for GCSE students. The goal of this has been to try and stop plagiarism from occurring and to encourage people to do more coursework at school.

How difficult are GCSEs?

Difficulty is always going to be relative. Some children will thrive at GCSE. Some will struggle with the demands placed upon them. How difficult your child finds the GCSE programme is something you are going to have to discuss with them.

There are, however, a few factors that might affect how well your child copes with the transition from Year 9 to GCSE studies in Years 10 and 11.

General academic ability

By the time your child is ready to study for GCSE, you should have a pretty good idea of where they fall in terms of their academic ability. As we have already said, some students just enjoy studying and enjoy taking exams, doing coursework, and taking on challenges of an academic nature. Others do not, either because they don't enjoy what they are doing or because they genuinely struggle. Students with specific learning disabilities, such as dyslexia and certain sensory processing disorders, may receive additional support at GCSE. If you are concerned that your child may need special educational support to cope with the academic demands at GCSE, it is a good idea to meet with the head of your child's school or the person otherwise designated to handle these issues.

Interest in school

Your child's level of interest in school is going to play a very important role in determining how well they cope with GCSEs. As we said previously, some students thrive when they are challenged academically. If your child is one of these types of students, the chances are good that they have a high level of interest and investment in their school experience and they want to do well.

If, on the other hand, your child has not found school to be interesting or engaging, they may very well withdraw during the GCSE process and therefore struggle – not because they have any academic or cognitive impairment but because they are simply not invested in the work.

Interest in subject matter

GCSE choices are crucially important to ensure that your child has every opportunity to do well at this stage in their education. Of the subjects your child can choose to study, they must pick subjects that interest them and that they will get good grades in.

Usually the two go hand in hand, but this is why it is important to talk to your child and their teachers about what subjects they should consider studying. The final decision is down to your child, but your role is to make sure that they have all the information they need to make the right decision.

Time management skills

GCSEs are demanding. There is no way around it. Your child is expected to prepare for examination in about ten subjects. They are also expected to prepare for multiple exams in each subject. They are even expected to take responsibility for much of their education at this stage.

'By the time your child is ready to study for GCSE, you should have a pretty good idea of where they fall in terms of their academic ability.'

Although you and their teachers are going to be invested in their work – in how well they prepare and how well they do in their exams – they are the ones that have to perform on exam day. They are also the ones who have to produce their coursework on time. They also have to take charge of their revision during study leave, which we will talk about in more detail later.

Because of these increased demands on your child and the reality that they are expected to be responsible for managing them, it becomes extremely important that they learn how to manage their time.

Teach your child how to manage their time if they don't already know. Time management skills can be learned quickly but they do need to be taught properly.

School environment and support

Your child's school – their teachers, their peers, and other support persons associated with the school – is going to be important to your child's GCSE success, too. A good school doesn't have to be the most expensive or the most prestigious. What makes a school 'good' for your child at GCSE is their level of comfort and degree of support. Passionate, dedicated and knowledgeable teachers are going to make all the difference to the outcome of your child's exams. This is why it is important to make sure that your child is comfortable in their school and feels that they have adequate support and a good staff of teachers to work with during their GCSE courses.

'Your child's school – their teachers, their peers, and other support persons associated with the school – is going to be important to your child's GCSE success'

What is the parent's role during the GCSE experience?

A parent's input during their child's GCSE experience can vary considerably depending on a couple of factors. Most obviously, it varies based on the parent-child relationship and the maturity and independence of the child.

In other words, if your child is particularly independent and mature in the way that they handle their schoolwork, it is unlikely that you will need to have a particularly 'hands-on' approach at GCSE. On the other hand, if your child enjoys, benefits from, or outright needs your direct involvement in their school life, you may find yourself very involved in every aspect of your child's GCSE experience.

There is no right or wrong answer to how much direct involvement you should have. The key is to provide your child as much support as they want and need. Keep the lines of communication open to make sure that you are providing the right amount and type of support. It should be a two-way process, of course. There are going to be limits as to what you can do. But, as we will emphasise throughout this book, communication is going to help resolve a lot of these issues.

Summing Up

- The General Certificate of Secondary Education examinations (GCSEs) are important for your child's future, both in school and beyond.

- Your child will likely be taking 10 subjects in preparation for GCSE examination, taught over two years when they are aged 14 to 16 and in Years 10 and 11.

- The difficulty of the GCSE process is going to vary depending on factors such as your child's academic abilities and knowledge in each subject; their interest in school and in the individual subjects they study; and the support they receive at school and at home.

- To help your child through their GCSE experience, the most important thing you can do is communicate. Open communication will help minimise potential problems and maximise your child's opportunities for success.

Chapter Two

Preparing for GCSEs Before Year 10: The Right School and Strategy

Why you should review secondary schools in preparation for GCSEs

Most parents confront the secondary school decision around Year 4 or Year 5. Many worry about the decision earlier than that. By the time your child is in Year 6, however, it is definitely time to make a decision about what secondary school is right for your child.

Before Year 6, if you are anxious about selecting a secondary school, concentrate on keeping things in perspective. While it may be advantageous to have a good idea about which school your child is likely to go to, it is not really necessary, or even particularly important, to know which school they are going to go to for their secondary education.

However, you should consider looking at secondary schools with a view to understanding what your child's options are going to be at GCSE and how well supported they are going to be by the time they are going through their GCSE examinations. The reason for this is simple. There is continuity between Years 7 to 9 and Years 10 to 11. Having your child supported in the same learning environment from age 11 onwards is consistent with the way that the education system is structured in the UK. Avoiding unnecessary transitions is ideal and what you should be aiming for. So picking a secondary school that is going to be the best place for your child, at least until the end of GCSEs, will provide the benefit of consistency. Your child will have the chance to get to know their teachers and to get to know what resources are available through the school. Teachers and other staff will also have the opportunity to get to know your child and what their interests, skills and needs are.

Factors to consider when reviewing school options for GCSE

There are several factors to consider when reviewing school options for GCSE, whether you are looking to make a decision with your child at the end of Year 9, transitioning midway through secondary school, or as early as the end of Year 6.

The type of school

The first factor to consider, when looking at school options, is the type of school you are looking at. There are, throughout the UK, several different types of schools that include independent or private schools, grammar schools, or comprehensive or secondary schools that are state-run and free.

Cost of schooling

The cost of sending your child to a good school can be either direct, indirect, or both. Independent schools are fee-based. State-run grammar schools and comprehensives or state-run secondary schools don't have direct costs (at least not any that are particularly significant). Indirect costs, though, can include high living costs in catchment areas for good secondary schools and grammar schools. This indirect cost can apply to all types of schools, including independent schools.

Selectivity of schools/Entry requirements

State-funded grammar secondary schools have entrance exams that prospective students are required to pass in order to have a placement. Most independent or private schools also select students based on entrance test results. Whether your child is able to pass entrance exams is going to be an important consideration in the selection of their secondary school. Because of the focus on academic ability, you may also find that your child will have less control over their GCSE subject selection because of an emphasis on a particular style of education.

Catchment/Location factors

Having your child attend a high-quality state secondary school may be a priority but it is going to be important to make sure that you are in a good catchment area. If you are not in the catchment area for your top choice school (or your child's top choice), weigh up the pros and cons of having your child at their second or third choice school (especially at GCSEs) versus possibly relocating into the right catchment area.

Special needs

Children with special needs require special support but the needs vary dramatically from one child to the next and will certainly affect the kind of support systems that work for them at GCSEs.

If your child has special needs, make sure you set up time to talk to your top choices in some detail about how they will be able to support your child's needs through the challenges of GCSEs.

It is important to ascertain whether your top choice of schools have experience with children with similar special needs. Because of the stress that is typically associated with GCSEs, not to mention the academic demands, it is important to ensure that your child's teachers understand all of their learning needs and know how to meet them effectively,

Your child's preferences

Perhaps the most important factor is your child and their requirements. Every child is an individual and is going to thrive in a different academic environment. You should take the time to talk with your child about the type of school experience that they want and the type of learning environment that they feel is going to be best for them, given that they understand about the demands of GCSE.

If you are considering switching schools or if you are looking at secondary schools ahead of time, it is important that you visit the schools to get a first-hand sense of whether you feel the environment is right for your child.

Depending on their education stage, you can always transfer within the school system when your child is ready to study GCSEs. If you feel like your child needs additional help they may not be able to get from school, there is always the option of going outside of school, too. If extra support may be helpful to your child, consider finding a tutoring company with experience of all school systems.

'Every child is an individual and is going to thrive in a different academic environment.'

Is it worth putting your child in private school to get better GCSE results?

Whether your child is in Year 6 and you are thinking ahead, or they are in Year 9 and on the brink of GCSEs, transfer to a private school is always going to be an option. Of course, if you decide you would prefer to have your child to go a private school or a grammar school, you will need to have them undertake the relevant testing.

For students in Year 6, entrance tests tend to take place in January. If your child is already in secondary school, testing is probably more flexible but it is still another step to organise.

The advantage of independent or grammar schools, for many children, is that they provide an opportunity for intensive academic study. The disadvantages include cost, most obviously. There are, however, no guarantees. As with any school you are considering for your child, especially when your focus is on GCSEs, look at as many factors as you can. These should include, above all, your child's preferences, the subjects available for GCSE, what subjects are considered compulsory at the school (how Year 10 and Year 11 are structured), and what type of supports are in place for GCSE students.

Where to get more information on school options for GCSE

General information on GCSEs is available online at http://www.direct.gov.uk/en/EducationAndLearning/QualificationsExplained/DG_10039024. On this website, you can find information on how to access local prospectuses to find out what subjects are available at GCSE in your area. This should give you an idea of which schools offer which subjects at GCSE.

How to prepare your child for GCSEs before Year 10

There are several things you can do to help prepare your child for their GCSEs before Year 10. Most of these things are simple, and many you probably do already without even thinking.

Encourage your child to think about their future

First, but perhaps not most obvious, is to encourage your child to consider their future. Implementing this strategy doesn't mean you push your child to make any career decisions, to decide on their university choices, or what they want to study. You don't even need to push your child to consider A level or GCSE choices before Year 10. Even in a year, people change. Children and teenagers in particular, go through a lot of change – physical, emotional, psychological. Their interests, wants, needs, and even their abilities, are likely to fluctuate. The point of thinking about the future before Year 10, is not to have your child decide on what they are going to do but to have them begin to realise that what they do – every decision they make in school and in life – is important. The goal is to have your child become invested in their future. Far better than having to make GCSEs and schoolwork a priority for your child, is to have them see the importance of these things for themselves.

'The point of thinking about the future before Year 10, is not to have your child decide on what they are going to do but to have them begin to realise that what they do – every decision they make in school and in life – is important.'

Perhaps the best way to get your child invested, too, is just to talk about the future and the possibilities that are before them.

Make schoolwork a priority

Although it need not be the only thing to have priority in your child's life, certainly by the time they enter secondary school, schoolwork and homework should be treated as important and necessary parts of life.

The more disciplined your child is about homework and schoolwork, the easier it will be for them to transition into Year 10. The easier it will be for them to make progress in their GCSE courses, juggling the workload for each course and, at the same time, finding time for the other things they enjoy and need to do.

'The more disciplined your child is about homework and schoolwork, the easier it will be for them to transition into Year 10.'

Instil good working habits

Part of having schoolwork be a priority is having good work habits and time management skills. Unfortunately, these are skills that do have to be taught. While some schools do make a solid effort to help students be responsible about their work, encouraging them to have a system for recording and prioritising assignments – a to-do list of sorts – it is certainly beneficial for parents to reinforce any such encouragement and even build on it.

When your child is in secondary school, before they reach Year 10, take the time to help them develop a schedule for after school time. This schedule can allow for extracurricular activities such as sports and music practices, but it should also clearly outline a time each day (or whenever they have homework) for your child to work without interruption or distraction.

Another important component for good working habits is a functional working environment. Have your child get into the habit of doing their homework at a desk, without the television or radio on in the background. Encourage them to keep this work environment tidy and clutter-free. Perhaps consider incorporating some time management or organisational tools in the work area, such as a calendar or cork board that will allow your child to post notes and reminders about assignments etc.

A clock or timer is also a good idea to ensure that your child gets into the habit of working for a certain length of time on each assignment. A timer can also help to incorporate all-important breaks into your child's work schedule; a habit that will, so long as it is used effectively, provide a number of benefits while your child is actually working towards their GCSEs.

Encourage a healthy lifestyle

Believe it or not, healthy eating and getting plenty of exercise – a balanced life – have an important impact on your child's overall happiness. You probably already know and appreciate this. In preparation for GCSEs, though, it is helpful to revisit this key point as early as you can – once your child is installed at secondary school and perhaps beginning to be more independent at home, socially, academically, and even emotionally.

It can be very productive to sit down and talk to your child about the need for balance in their lives. If they don't already have a hobby or some extracurricular interests, as your child enters secondary school, and thus a whole new phase of their lives, it could be very useful to revisit pointers such as healthy eating, personal care, exercise, extracurricular activities and social commitments.

Be supportive

A child's transition towards GCSEs can be a very challenging time and, although it may go unnoticed for a while, even several years, the transition really starts quite early on in your child's education. By Year 7, it's fairly safe to say that your child is on their way towards GCSEs based on the way the current system works. It is important to recognise that your child may be realising the importance of the work they are doing in school – how important it is for their own future. As a parent, you know your role, much of the time, is to be your child's advocate and supporter, helping them to wrestle through challenges. It is no different en route to GCSE studies.

Support your child early on, through their transition to secondary school and throughout the period at secondary school leading up to GCSEs. Establish grounds for open communication.

'The point of thinking about the future before Year 10, is not to have your child decide on what they are going to do but to have them begin to realise that what they do – every decision they make in school and in life – is important.'

Allow your child the opportunity to let you know how they feel about school and what they feel they might like to do in school as it becomes time to think about GCSE and even A level choices.

Ask your child whether they feel well supported in their current learning environment, whether there are any areas in which they feel they are struggling academically. Are there any skills sets they want to work on developing? Are there subjects that they would like to study?

Summing Up

- If possible, the school your child goes to in Year 7 should be selected based, at least, in part on the GCSE options that will be available to them from Years 10 and 11. Plan ahead!

- Picking a secondary school, you should consider your child's needs in the context of resources that are available. Is your child going to be adequately supported in the school environment?

- Weigh up the pros and cons of state schools versus independent schools, comprehensives versus grammar schools. Remember, every child is different and at the end of the day, your child is the one who is going to be in the school.

- Visit prospective schools and ask about the systems they have in place to support students at GCSE.

- Talk to your child about their interests and what they think they might like to study at GCSE. They can certainly change their mind but having some idea of their interests is going to help you make an informed decision about what might be the best environment.

- It is never too early for you and your child to be thinking about GCSE choices, about the transition to GCSE, and about your child's interests and goals in school, which may play a role in determining their future career choices.

- Although they do not have to make any decisions before Year 10 about what they want to study, you should encourage your child to think about GCSE options and even perhaps A level options and university or job interests past Year 11 or Year 13 if they plan to go through the A level process.

- Helping your child at this phase in their education can be as simple as encouraging them to make schoolwork a priority.

Chapter Three

Choosing GCSE Subjects

What subjects are available at GCSE?

There are more than 40 academic subjects that your child can study at GCSE and nine so-called 'applied' subjects.

An applied subject relates to an area of 'work'. They include subjects such as engineering or tourism. For students who are interested in going into employment after GCSE, these may be particularly useful qualifications to obtain as many of them are considered to be especially valuable – worth double the size of traditional GCSEs according to some.

GCSE subjects are also available as full or short courses. Short courses are the equivalent of half of a full GCSE. They are designed to be completed within half the time although they can be spread over a short course over the same length as a traditional GCSE.

What subjects are compulsory at GCSE?

There are several subjects that are compulsory at GCSE and it is important for you and your child to be aware of what they are and what their study entails, for a couple of reasons.

First of all, you need to be aware of these compulsory subjects so you can make sure your child is aware of them. Different people excel at different subjects. It is important, at the very least, that your child puts in a reasonable effort for these compulsory subjects, however, because there is no way around taking examinations in these subjects at GCSE.

'There are more than 40 academic subjects that your child can study at GCSE and nine so-called "applied" subjects.'

Compulsory subjects at GCSE include:

- English.
- Mathematics.
- Science (usually taught as Dual Degree).

Although the majority of subjects your child will study are going to lead to examinations, there are also a number of so-called compulsory subjects that may not lead to exams but are nonetheless required for study at GCSE.

These subjects include:

- Careers education.
- Citizenship.
- Information and communication technology (ICT).
- Physical education (PE).
- Religious studies (RS) – sometimes referred to as religious education.

'There are a number of optional subjects that your child may be able to take in Years 10 and 11.'

There are a number of optional subjects that your child may be able to take in Years 10 and 11. These are divided into four 'entitlement areas' and each school must offer students the opportunity to study at least one subject from each of these categories.

The entitlement areas are:

- Arts.
- Design and technology.
- Humanities.
- Modern foreign languages.

Arts include the following subjects:

- Art and design.
- Music.
- Dance.
- Drama and media arts.

Humanities include the following subjects:

- History.
- Geography.

Modern foreign languages include the following subjects:

- French.
- German.
- Spanish.

Depending on your child's school, your child may also be able to choose from some of the following subjects in addition to those that are considered compulsory and in addition to those that fit within the four 'entitlement areas':

- Business studies.
- Engineering.
- Health and social care.
- Leisure and tourism.
- Social sciences.

These various subjects may be taught at your school and known by a different name. If there is a subject that your child wants to study, it is worth asking whether the subject is available for study at their school.

How do you find out what subjects are available at your child's school?

Many schools post information on available GCSE subjects online and by far the easiest way to find out about what subjects are available for study in your area is to use the website Directgov pertaining to 'Where Are You Heading?' Here you can search via postcode, street and town, or local authority.

'Where Are You Heading?' website: http://yp.direct.gov.uk/14-19prospectus/

Picking GCSE options

The selection of GCSE subjects, these days, is at least a two-step process.

When it comes to the selection of subjects, however, your child has the final say. At least, they are the ones who have to formally make the selections. Your role, as parent, is to provide appropriate guidance and, perhaps even more significantly, serve as a sounding board for the various options your child may be weighing up.

Help your child choose a subject they will enjoy

This is a first principle for your child's GCSE selection – that they choose a subject they will enjoy.

In fact, this might be the golden rule for any sort of decision-making along these lines. If you enjoy a subject, you are more likely to do well. Trying to learn something – a subject – that you do not enjoy is quite often a demoralising experience, one that leaves you struggling to make a good grade.

Whatever your child's career goals, it is important to realise it may well be better for them to take a GCSE subject they enjoy, that they can do well in, rather than try to pick a subject that they feel they ought to take, for whatever reason.

It is important, though, to make an informed decision based on an understanding of what the GCSE course will involve.

You can help your child here by having them think not only about the skills required by a given subject but also about the programme of study for GCSE. Talk to them about the course of study in particular and make sure that the topics they will have to study are going to be of interest. Remember that with subjects such as history, geography, English literature and so on, the content of the course is going to be different from what your child is used to, even after studying the same subject in previous years. The skills required may also be different from GCSE to A level so make sure that your child's interest in a given subject is likely to hold up at GCSE as you look to apply this first principle.

'Whatever your child's career goals, it is important to realise it may well be better for them to take a GCSE subject they enjoy, that they can do well in, rather than try to pick a subject that they feel they ought to take, for whatever reason.'

Need2Know

If your child is thinking about trying a new subject altogether because it sounds interesting or because they have an interest in the subject developed outside of school, find out more about the way the subject is taught at GCSE and how it is assessed. Just because your child wants to study something like psychology, law or politics doesn't mean that they are going to necessarily find the subject interesting as it is taught at GCSE. Make sure, if your child decides to pick a new subject that they understand what the course content is and how the subject is taught and examined. This way, you can make sure that the first principle is actually being followed appropriately and your child is picking a subject they are going to enjoy.

Help your child to choose subjects that fit their career plan

This is the second principle: that your child should choose subjects which will fit in with their career plans.

Although we have already discussed the extent to which future career plans should not tie your child's hands in GCSE course selection, it is important, particularly if they have a clear career path, to be aware of any requirements for university study of a given subject. There are many degree courses that require certain subjects for entry.

Talk to your child about their career plans and, even if they are tentative, make a list of possible degree subjects. With this list, go to the UCAS website www. ucas.ac.uk and check for any degree requirements.

Your school should also be able to offer some career advice and even certain forms of testing to help your child clarify their long-term plans. It may be a good idea to do this before your child finalises GCSE subjects, although your child shouldn't feel they have to make decisions at this point.

In fact, consistent with our second principle here, you should help your child to understand that it is generally – almost always, in fact – a bad idea to take a subject just because it is needed for a particular career. The only exception is when your child has good reason to believe that the subject is going to be easier at GCSE, based on a review of the course requirements and feedback from teachers.

'Careers can seem a long way off at GCSE but the choices your child makes now are going to influence their options in two years time, when they have GCSEs under their belt and are thinking about the next stage.'

Careers can seem a long way off at GCSE but the choices your child makes now are going to influence their options in two years time, when they have GCSEs under their belt and are thinking about the next stage.

Discuss subject options with people who know your child

This might seem like odd advice but it is all part of taking the time to find out as much as you can about your child's GCSE subject options and what will end up being the best choice for them. To help your child make the right choices, you should not only discuss the first two principles with them but encourage them to seek out advice from third parties. Have them talk to their advisor, the school's career advisor, and teachers of specific subjects that they are interested in or that you think they might enjoy studying.

Take time to find out all you need to know about their interests, skills, performance levels, and their preferred direction after GCSE. You can (and probably should) be transparent about demonstrating your interest. Make sure your child is aware who you are talking to. Since they are the principle decision-maker, the more you can do to reinforce your role as an advisor and advocate, the better. Encourage your child to come along with you to meet with careers advisors and teachers if you decide to make meetings outside of structured events like parents' evenings and open house nights.

The goal is give your child the time and information they need to talk to people, make decisions, and change their mind if necessary.

To help your child through the decision-making process, emphasise the importance of listening to other people and accepting that other people might have good advice and opinions worth considering. At the same time, though, help them understand that they are the person who must make the final decision because your child is the one who will be doing the work and living with these decisions.

Sources of information on GCSE subjects

To start collecting information about GCSE subjects and options for your child, look to the following resources:

GCSE subject guides

There are numerous subject guides for GCSE. Often these are a good starting point for parents looking to get a handle on the subjects their children are considering for GCSE. Obviously, these are good guidebooks for students, too. They should give an outline of content and skills needed and information on how a given subject is assessed. Most of these guides also go into detail on things like subject combination restrictions.

It is likely your child will find many of these sorts of books in their local library or in the general library of their school.

Some websites provide online student subject guides, too. If it proves difficult to find relevant books, or if you are finding some of the information outdated or limited, turning to the Internet may be a good idea.

Teachers past and present

Beyond books, good sources of information on appropriate subjects for your child at GCSE are their current and past teachers.

Any competent teacher who has worked with your child should have a good knowledge of their intellectual strengths and weaknesses not to mention a sense of their general skills and knowledge foundation.

As you are helping your child to work out which subjects they want to study, it is certainly a good idea to ask their teachers – current teachers and any past teachers you and your child particularly trust – about what subjects they think might be a good fit. Having past and current teachers review GCSE selections is also a good idea to help confirm that your child is making the right choice based on their abilities.

Specifications for GCSE subjects

Yet another excellent resource for you and your child are the GCSE specifications, sometimes called exam board syllabuses. These documents are published by each exam board for the GCSE subjects and they describe the topics to be covered for each course.

'Yet another excellent resource for you and your child are the GCSE specifications, sometimes called exam board syllabuses.'

Note that these documents are also a good resource for your child's revision because they are often very detailed in their description of the knowledge and skills your child is supposed to demonstrate.

There are three main exam boards that you need to be aware of:

- AQA.

- Edexcel.

- OCR.

You will need to determine which exam board is used by your school. You can find exam board syllabuses for full and short course requirements for each GCSE subject online at the three main exam board websites.

Other students

Just as you should encourage your child to speak to other sixth-formers or those who have recently finished their GCSE courses about the GCSE experience, encourage them to talk to these same types of people about subject choices.

Have your child talk to GCSE students who are currently studying the subjects they are considering.

Questions to ask include:

- What do you like best about the subject in general?

- What do you like best about the GCSE course?

- What do you dislike about the course?

- What have you found to be (the most) challenging?

Texts and reference books

As your child is reviewing syllabuses for courses they are interested in and also talking to people who have studied certain subjects at GCSE, it may be a good idea to encourage them to review the textbooks and reference books used to reach the subjects they are interested in.

Having your child skim through these books is another way to give them a sense of the type of work that they would be doing if they opt for any given course. Reviewing textbooks and reference books can also be particularly useful when they are considering choosing a subject that they have never studied before, as these sources can give a sense of how the subject is going to be taught.

Considering GCSE requirements for A levels and beyond

There are few hard and fast rules about GCSE requirements for A levels or thereafter for specific degrees. In most cases, if your child has good grades and some general evidence of their interest in a given subject, they have as good a shot as anyone to be accepted for any undergraduate major of their choice. However, there are a few exceptions with degrees like veterinary sciences, dentistry, pharmaceuticals or biology. Anyone interested in a career in these areas is expected to opt for full GCSEs in sciences (most particularly, in biology and chemistry). At the very least, these are logical choices for anyone considering these kinds of careers.

For a degree in law, it is useful (but again, not required) to have a range of subjects demonstrating cognitive ability and the ability to write. This same standard is going to be expected at A level but universities are going to look at GCSE results for two things – demonstrated ability and demonstrated interest.

Anyone considering a course in European business studies or similar is strongly recommended to pursue an A level in a European language (French, German, Spanish, primarily). Taking at least one language is important at GCSE but it may be a better idea to take two languages at GCSE to leave your options open at A level and also to establish the pattern of interested from GCSE to A level.

Prospective psychology majors also do well to have a mix of arts/humanities subjects and the sciences.

As a general rule:

'Universities are going to look at GCSE results for two things – demonstrated ability and demonstrated interest.'

- Most degree courses expect at least one subject that is strongly demonstrative of your child's interest in the degree course (e.g. study history at GCSE and A level if you want to study it at university)

- Top academic degree courses usually require three solid academic A levels (so no courses like psychology, business studies, law at A level) but they will also be looking for strong GCSEs.

Summing Up

- There are more than 40 academic subjects that your child can study at GCSE level and nine so-called 'applied' subjects.

- Your child will have several core subjects that are considered compulsory. They will also have a choice of about five subjects to choose from as optional.

- Choosing the right subjects at GCSE depends on interest and ability; your child should pick subjects they are interested in and they should also pick subjects that they are good at.

- Career interests should also play a role in GCSE subject selection, although not necessarily a huge one unless you child is considering leaving school at 16 to pursue a career or vocational training.

Chapter Four

Helping Your Child to Balance Time and Build Skill Sets Through Years 10 and 11

Defining time management for GCSE students

One of the biggest challenges for parents of GCSE students is communication. Just as you may have filtered the advice thrown at you when you were their age, your child, throughout Year 10 and Year 11, is striving for independence. Part of this may very well mean trying things on their own. It may mean that they have what some parents jokingly refer to as 'selective hearing'. Unless you approach things like time management directly and in a collaborative, open manner, your child may not pick up that you are simply trying to be helpful – trying to help them be more independent and effective workers.

The first step to overcoming any potential communication problem, however, is to offer a clear definition of what 'time management' is. Although your child probably has at least a basic idea of what time management is all about – they have probably been working with timetables and homework diaries for a while, prioritising homework and so forth – it is still common for teenagers approaching their GCSEs to struggle with it. In fact, many professional adults struggle with time management. By helping your child with this area of their GCSE experience, you are actually helping them prepare for challenges that

'One of the biggest challenges for parents of GCSE students is communication.'

they are going to face throughout their lives, not just at GCSE but certainly at A level and university if they decide to go on to higher education. Even if your child decides to start work after completing their GCSEs, or opts for another technical path, they are still going to need to be able to manage their time effectively. They will be able to accomplish so much more when they have mastered this one skill.

But what is time management?

Quite simply, it is the application of certain principles or systems to organise and use time effectively. Often, it goes hand in hand with goal management designed to help a person prioritise what they need to work on at any given time.

Since everyone is different, time management and goal management system selection often involves trial and error to find out which approach will work best.

Helping your child create and stick to a schedule

Not only does everyone work in different ways, every teenager has different demands placed upon them these days.

The minute-to-minute details of your child's schedule are going to be determined by their schooling demands, extracurricular demands, family demands and social demands.

The first step to identifying the minute-to-minute details, however, is to have your child write a list of things they do on a daily basis, e.g. wake up, take a shower, go to school, do homework, do chores, etc.

The second step is to write a list of the things your child needs to do on a weekly basis. This list might include things like extracurricular activities, sports activities and social activities.

A third list might include monthly activities and other special events.

With these three lists drawn up, you can then help your child to identify a single calendar system. The system could be online, set up somewhere like Google Calendars. In fact, this is a good idea because your child can set reminders and alarms for events, as well as create to-do lists.

If your child works better when they write things down, however, a planner would probably be best.

The most important point is that there needs to be a single system that is used consistently.

Tips for managing time

With a schedule and calendar in place, there are a few suggestions you can make to your child to maximise the effectiveness of the more basic time management system:

Track time

These days, it is very easy to set timers and keep a record of how your time is spent. It is easy enough to do on a computer or a mobile phone.

Tracking time, however, is really the first step to effective time management for anyone, including students.

Recording what you are doing, when and for how long, you get a sense of several things. First, you get a sense of how well you are managing your time. Second, you can also get a sense of whether you are effectively prioritising your time. Third, you can also check for and eliminate activities that are a waste of time.

Take regular breaks

To reduce stress and increase focus long term, it is a good idea to encourage your teenager to take regular breaks. Breaks might be up to about 15 minutes at a time and staggered throughout the day.

Effective breaks might involve focused breathing for several minutes at a time, even meditation.

If your child is the type of person who enjoys being outside, being able to walk about to clear their head might be effective too.

A break could simply be five or ten minutes spent getting a drink or a snack. The important thing is to find out what works for your child and make sure they apply the information.

Create homework time at school

Because it limits distractions, it is often a good idea for students to complete homework tasks at school rather than at home. Homework time at school could be during lunch or during break time.

Although most GCSE students don't have independent study periods, there may still be opportunities for them to complete some of their homework at school.

At the very least, your child should take time to manage their homework requirements – making a list of their homework in detail to ensure that they do the work accurately and effectively at home.

These are also ideal for homework time at school. And the more homework your child manages to complete at home, the more time they will have in the evening to fit in other activities, revision activities and relaxation time.

Prioritisation as a time management tool

Goal-setting fits in with time management as a system for organising what you need to get done each day, each week, each month. For GCSE, goal-setting or prioritisation of tasks will help your child manage their course load effectively.

Simple prioritisation strategies

The simplest and perhaps the easiest way to teach your child to prioritise tasks involves using a system for urgent, normal and low priority.

'Although most GCSE students don't have independent study periods, there may still be opportunities for them to complete some of their homework at school.'

If your child makes a list of their tasks for each period of time – every day, for instance – they can also get into the habit of marking tasks according to this priority scale.

- Urgent tasks are those that require immediate attention or are very important, such as, for instance, coursework pieces.

- Normal priority tasks are those that need to be completed but are less urgent or less important than, for instance, coursework or specific exam revision.

- Low priority tasks are those that can perhaps be put off for a day or so.

When it comes to dividing up their time, your child can then refer to their tasks according to priority. Setting aside the scheduled tasks that cannot be avoided, such as going to school, travelling to and from school, eating meals, that sort of thing, your child can work out how much time they have free to focus on different types of projects.

Tasks can then be divided up in the available time slots.

The 'top three tasks' approach for the overwhelmed student

For children that are really overwhelmed by the list of things they have to do – and most teenagers have a long list to work through – a good task management system might be the 'top three' approach. Instead of worrying about everything they need to try and do, encourage your child to write a daily list of the top three things they need to do from their general task list.

Concentrating on only these three things within the time they have available, anyone feeling overwhelmed can get a good handle on their work.

Setting a timer may also help to improve focus.

Most teenagers and adults can focus for about 45 minutes on a single task. Working on the top three tasks, encourage your child to work for intervals of 45 minutes, followed by a 5 to 15-minute break to complete homework or chores.

Not only will this approach help your child to manage their to-do list daily, it will also help instil good habits, preparing them to be that much more effective at university and beyond.

The 'Getting it Done' approach to stay motivated

If you really want to instil positive goal and task management for your child, teaching them to use a system like 'Getting it Done' might be something to consider.

Online you can find a whole range of resources related to this particular style of goal and task management.

If your child struggles to stay motivated to keep up with this kind of systematic planning, GID might also be a good choice because it really can be a fun exercise to use this system.

'The transition to Year 10 is perhaps the biggest challenge for students moving on to GCSE.'

What skills does your child need to succeed in Year 10?

The transition to Year 10 is perhaps the biggest challenge for students moving on to GCSE. The purpose of their education until this point, however, has been to prepare them to develop the skills that will be necessary at this point, to succeed at GCSE level.

The most important skills for GCSE success include the following:

- Critical thinking.
- Communication skills (written and verbal).
- Reasoning skills (problem-solving, decision-making).

While this looks pretty simple, the challenge for many Year 10 students is the level of expectation. Not only is your child expected to demonstrate these skills, they have to demonstrate them at a particular level.

In the study of English language or literature, for instance, your child will be expected to demonstrate the ability to think critically about the purpose of a text, analysing the context, the audience, the style and other components.

Analysis will have to be undertaken on both in a broad sense, applied to an entire text, but also in a very specific context, looking sometimes at specific words or specific sections of a text.

Your child will also be expected to communicate their ideas about their critical reasoning in an effective manner. They will have to learn to be especially clear and concise in their written communication as well as in verbal communication (delivering presentations, for instance, which is often a component of GCSE study).

In the study of mathematics at GCSE, your child will be expected to demonstrate the ability to problem-solve at a fairly high level, too. They will be introduced to abstract mathematical concepts in their study of algebra and geometry at GCSE that will require this abstract reasoning and problem-solving.

Beyond these skills, your child will also have to hone their time management skills, their study skills, and their exam-taking skills to succeed at GCSE, although there is generally more time for them to develop these skills as they are not absolutely needed until Year 11.

What can you do to help your child manage the transition to GCSE level?

The best way to help your child manage the transition to GCSE is outlined throughout this book – by supporting your child and working to understand the components of the experience of GCSE study and examination, you are well on your way to supporting their transition to GCSE level.

Because every child is different, you will have to make a determination, beyond this, as to what you can do to support your child's transition. If they need additional academic support – if they have struggled academically in the past or if they simply lack confidence in their abilities – organising for tutoring may be useful. It is worth remembering that GCSE does require that your child undertake core subjects, not all of which are going to be of interest. Your child may also struggle in any one of the core subject areas.

What skills does your child need to have for GCSE exam success?

Beyond the straightforward academic skills, your child is going to need to develop exam skills for GCSE.

Although your child will not be unfamiliar with formal test-taking having completed Key Stage 3 assessments in Year 9, the demand at GCSE is higher. Whatever subject your child is taking, there are going to be certain exam techniques your child will have to work on over Year 10 and Year 11.

In English language or literature, for instance, or in humanities subjects such as history or geography, your child will have to learn to write concise essays that effectively communicate ideas that can also be supported by a reasonable amount of evidence. Your child will also have to learn how to organise evidence for analysis.

'Beyond the straightforward academic skills, your child is going to need to develop exam skills for GCSE.'

The best way to support this development, though, is also to be supportive of your child throughout Year 10 and Year 11, emphasising the importance of schoolwork and, if necessary, helping them to access additional supports (tutors, study guides, etc.) to support their own efforts undertaken with the support of teachers.

How can you help your child develop the necessary skills for exam success?

The development of skills for exams is somewhat less pressing at GCSE than the development of other core skills. Your child will likely have until Year 11 to really master effective exam strategies.

What do these strategies include?

The main skills include:

- Learning to read and break down the components of exam questions.
- Time management within the context of an exam.
- Learning to break down the time available in an exam to answer specific questions or sections for questions.

- Learning to check and recheck work.

Other subjects, such as foreign languages, require your child to develop certain other skills, such as the ability to prepare the elements for verbal responses to questions (for oral examinations).

The best way to help your child develop all of the necessary exam skills, though, is still to provide general support throughout Year 10 and Year 11. Supporting your child's efforts at school will help them to make use of the information that is communicated to them by their teachers. It will also help them to make the most of the skills that their various teachers work to help them develop.

By taking an active role in your child's school experience throughout Years 10 and 11, communicating with teachers and helping your child to meet their individual needs (e.g. by helping them to access resources such as tutors or study guides), you give them their best opportunity to be successful and learn these skills.

Helping them through their revision period, perhaps by monitoring their efforts to take practice exams, you can also help your child to learn to put these skills into practice and master them by the time they get to their actual GCSE exam period.

'By taking an active role in your child's school experience throughout Years 10 and 11, communicating with teachers, and helping your child to meet their individual needs you give them their best opportunity to be successful and learn these skills.'

Summing Up

- Your child is expected to develop certain skills for GCSEs.

- Time management and study skills are going to be important.

- Those skills form the basis of most testing at GCSE and fall under general categories such as critical thinking and reasoning.

- Exam success is also dependent upon how well your child masters certain skills such as time management and question break down under time pressure.

- The best way to help your child develop the skills required for GCSE success is to be supportive of their school experience in general and to look out for other ways to meet their individual needs such as by making certain resources available to them or supporting their efforts to practise certain skills under exam-like conditions.

Chapter Five

Mock Exams, Coursework and Study Leave

What are mock exams?

Some time in Year 11, probably in January, your child will undertake what are known as mock exams.

Mock exams are designed to help your child and their teachers gauge what grade they are likely to earn in each GCSE subject.

The benefit of mock exams for you and your child is that they give a fairly good indication of areas where your child is on track to achieve good grades and where they might need to concentrate their revision to improve their expected grades.

What is coursework?

Exams go hand in hand with coursework at GCSE and also at A level.

Coursework could be anything from a lengthy written piece, to an experiment, to a piece of art work or a design project.

The type of coursework your child has to complete will depend on their course of study – both the subject and the exam board – and their GCSE option subjects.

In some instances, your child may have a choice as to whether they complete coursework or take an extra exam to demonstrate knowledge and skills relevant to a specific area of study.

'Mock exams are designed to help your child and their teachers gauge what grade they are likely to earn in each GCSE subject.'

Since coursework is also graded (at least initially) by your child's teacher in each subject, coursework is another way to gauge what grades your child may receive at GCSE.

Coursework can also be retaken if your child is unhappy with the results. Because coursework is often completed in Year 10, it can be advantageous to redo coursework in Year 11 if you know, for instance, that your child has developed new skills or honed other skills between Years 10 and 11. It is important to discuss redoing coursework with your child and their teacher, however, because the time involved can detract from other learning or revision, which could also affect your child's overall grade for GCSE.

What are the pros and cons of coursework?

'The advantage of coursework is that it provides your child the opportunity to demonstrate their knowledge and skills under less time pressure.'

The advantage of coursework is that it provides your child the opportunity to demonstrate their knowledge and skills under less time pressure. Coursework allows your child more time to plan and organise their thoughts as well as more time to prepare a project for submission.

Coursework is generally produced for the course subjects in the form of written work (research projects in science and mathematics or critical essays in English).

If your child has the option to choose coursework or an exam, the advantage of coursework is that they have one less exam to deal with. Many teachers recognise the advantage of this and so you may find that your child is completing coursework in a number of areas.

The disadvantage of coursework, though, is that sometimes it is extremely time-consuming. The stress of undertaking coursework in addition to the regular workload applied at GCSE may be detrimental.

Another factor can be the nature of coursework itself, that it tests skills that may be different from those tested in an exam scenario. Whereas you are likely to revise facts and practise specific ways of answering questions in preparation for examination under test conditions, with coursework, a broader range of skills may be tested, including skills related to project planning and creativity, not to mention time management and goal-setting – some skills we have mentioned earlier as being important for GCSE success.

Preparing for and monitoring performance across mock exams

Regardless of whether your child does better in exam settings or when working more independently and across a longer period of time, what you, as a parent, need to be most aware of with mock exams, is that they are not an absolute guarantee as far as results are concerned.

That said, with coursework grades (which will be supplied by your child's teachers) you and your child can have some idea as to how well they are going to perform overall.

Because not every exam or component of GCSE study is likely to be as easy as the others, another advantage of mock exams is that they provide your child with the means to figure out which areas of their revision should take priority.

It helps for them to be aware of what they are likely to struggle with both by subject and by subject area.

The results of mock exams can help your child plan and manage their revision time. They can also help your child determine whether it may be worthwhile to redo coursework modules.

'The results of mock exams can help your child plan and manage their revision time.'

What is study leave?

Study leave is a break from school. It is an opportunity to work at home (or anywhere else you choose that is not school).

Study leave usually begins a couple of weeks before exams begin. This means there is a good portion of time for you to set up a study schedule and really get some focused revision done.

GCSE is often the first opportunity for your child to experience study leave and take substantial control of and responsibility for their own work.

Why is it important?

One of the goals of the GCSE experience is to help students learn to be more independent and to have them take more personal accountability in their learning and in their work.

Provided they are sensible with this time (i.e. not using study leave as holiday time) then the major benefit of study leave is that it allows them to cut out a lot of time-wasting activity.

Time-wasting isn't just about sitting around on the couch playing video games, or talking on the phone. Daily activities including travel to and from school can be unduly time-wasting too, especially when your child is trying to use their time effectively to revise and prepare for exams.

'The secret to managing study leave effectively is to plan it – to know what time there is available to study and to figure out how to use that time effectively.'

What can you do to help your child use study leave effectively?

Everyone learns differently and everyone studies differently. Give your child some space to discover or rediscover what studying style works best for them, especially when it comes to study leave.

Generally speaking, the secret to managing study leave effectively is to plan it – to know what time there is available to study and to figure out how to use that time effectively. Since few teenagers are experts at time management, you can help your child prepare for exams by giving them guidance in this one area – planning their time.

The best way to manage study leave is with planning and scheduling tools that are designed to manage time effectively – a calendar/schedule and a timer.

As we've already suggested, helping your child to manage time with schedules and calendars will help them to learn time management skills and goal-setting for the purpose of prioritisation. When they master these skills, they will be in a position to manage study leave effectively.

However, when it comes to study leave, you should also be ready to help your child with managing stress.

If you find your child is spending their study leave buried in books, working flat out with no breaks, no time to relax, you should try to help them rethink their approach.

Why? Because overworking the body and brain is as problematic for exam success as underworking it. If your child is spending their time wrapped up in exam preparation and revision, they are not effectively addressing other needs – the need to rest, the need to relax, the need to eat, etc.

Remember that the most successful students, without exception, are the ones who develop structured, productive, balanced routines for their schoolwork and revision. They give themselves enough time to sleep properly, time to get some exercise, time to relax and have fun, and time to work.

Time management suggestions

Although everyone works differently, as a general rule, early morning and early afternoon are good times to undertake more intensive revision and work. The afternoon and early evening times are generally better for less intense revision, including background reading. However, if they decide to undertake less demanding revision work at this time, they may want to think about having a coffee on hand because this is also a time of day in which people become quite drowsy. Other options you can encourage are (1) taking a break to get some exercise or (2) getting a carbohydrate boost – a banana or another healthy carbohydrate snack to jolt their energy and overall alertness.

What strategies are particularly effective for studying during this break?

First of all, your child needs goals and a timetable or schedule to work with and you may be able to help them with this aspect of their revision.

To help your child set up a schedule, consider providing them access to timetabling tools such as calendars or planners. Online calendars or planners are particularly useful.

Help your child to create a reasonable schedule allowing between 6 and 10 hours of revision per day. This will give your child ample time to work on their revision and to set aside time for other things (sleeping, eating, relaxing, community activities, etc.).

The best way you can help them to set goals is by helping them identify the components of an effective goal.

Generally, it is a good idea to develop goals using the SMART technique:

A classic technique for goal-setting and management is SMART. It's used by many of the world's top organisations to assess the nature of your goals. According to the SMART programmes, your goals should be:

- **S**pecific – Have they clearly defined their goal?

- **M**easurable – How will they know if they are making progress?

- **A**chievable – Is their goal really achievable? They should be ambitious but honest.

- **R**ewarding – Is their goal something they are willing to make sacrifices for?

- **T**imely – Is their goal achievable in a meaningful timeframe?

Once your child has an effective schedule in place and workable goals, the last thing you can do to help them is to ensure that they are using study leave effectively: make sure that their study approach is an effective one.

'No one can revise what they have not learned in the first place.'

Reviewing syllabuses and learned materials

Before your child starts revising, it is important that they go through the list of topics pertaining to their course of study, reviewing the elements that need to be covered based on the syllabus.

First, no one can revise what they have not learned in the first place.

The first thing your child needs to check is that they have actually learned everything that is going to be or could be covered in the exam. It they feel there are things they haven't learned, one thing you can do is help them to access study guides or other materials to fill in any gaps in their knowledge.

Ideally, your child should have at least one copy of their course syllabus to look at before starting their revision in earnest. Most of these documents are available online in their latest edition so you can help your child by printing off a couple of copies. They should go through a copy of their syllabus for each subject with a highlighter to identify areas that they feel they have not yet covered in class.

Another thing they can do once they have identified any actual gaps in their learning, is go through a copy of the syllabus with a couple of different coloured highlighters.

You can support your child's organisation of their syllabus with the following technique:

They should try using three different highlighters – a red or pink highlighter, an orange highlighter, and a green highlighter.

They need to designate these colours with a specific value.

- Red can indicate a topic or a key point – an element of the syllabus – that they feel they are going to have to incorporate as a priority in their revision. For instance, if they feel that they really do not have a solid grasp of a specific concept that is a component of their syllabus, they can highlight references to the concept in red, indicating that this is material that they need to concentrate on in their revision.

- Orange can indicate topics or key points that they are relatively familiar with but feel that they still need to work on quite a bit.

- They can use a green highlighter for topics or key concepts that they are particularly comfortable with.

If you feel your child could use support applying this technique, it may be worthwhile to help them through the process, working with them.

Organise learning materials

Once your child has highlighted specific topics and prioritised them with colour-coding, they need to create some kind of database for organising the topics they need to cover in their revision and the learning materials they have to work with, to review, in order to cover them.

One way to do this is to create a kind of database.

First, your child should think about making a list of topics and keywords from the syllabus of each subject they are working on.

They should then list learning materials by categories.

In most instances, your child is going to have books and articles to work with, as well as textbooks, class notes, handbooks from teachers and other resources. If you think it is warranted, you may want to consider buying study guides or other support tools to help your child with their revision.

For each topic and keyword, your child should make a list of the learning materials that are going to be relevant.

It is important that all the relevant class notes and learning materials are collected and organised before revision starts. You may be able to help your child with this – helping them to put any books they need on hand.

To organise their learning materials effectively, you may want to help your child to create a database from the revision topics they have outlined.

'To organise their learning materials effectively, you may want to help your child to create a database from the revision topics they have outlined.'

Prioritise learning topics

Ideally, your child should also have access to past papers or exam questions for the last two to three years. This will allow them to see which topics covered on the syllabuses have have already come up in exams.

At the very least, knowing what has already been covered will help your child to prioritise topics for revision. This is also something you can help with simply by lending a hand during the process or otherwise making sure that your child undertakes this prioritisation process properly.

Help your child to identify the most productive time of day

Encourage your child to think about what time of day they work most effectively. Some people work best early in the morning. Others work best late at night. Some are more alert and more effective during the afternoon.

Your child will have to figure out what time of day works best for their revision. They will also have to figure out what period of time works best for them.

The time period that works best for your child is going to be determined by their concentration span – and everyone's concentration span varies.

If your child is easily distracted, then they should keep revision sessions short – about forty minutes – taking short breaks between those periods so that their concentration does not suffer. Providing them with a timer – even an egg timer will do – can help with the management of time intervals.

If your child has a good concentration span, working for up to an hour on a given subject may be fine. It can also be appropriate for your child to block off a couple of hours (up to two) of back-to-back study, avoiding any possible overloading of the concentration span. They can follow this up with at least a short break, although longer breaks can be allowed.

Helping your child to identify the most effective revision techniques

As we've said, everyone studies differently. Different revision techniques are going to work for your child versus everyone else. It is also up to your child, for the most part, to figure out what techniques work best for them.

Some techniques you can suggest, though, include the following:

* Note taking.
* Revision cards.
* Diagrams and charts.
* Group or paired revision.

Note taking

Note taking is by far the most common form of revision but it is generally not enough, by itself, to constitute effective revision for GCSE exams.

'If your child is easily distracted, then they should keep revision sessions short.'

If your child decides to use note taking as a revision strategy, they should be focusing on reviewing course materials – class notes, textbooks, etc. – and rehashing the information to constitute notes that are easy to memorise. You can help with this process by overseeing the way that they convert their notes.

One way to maximise the effectiveness of note taking, though, is to catalogue information in several different ways. Keywords and concepts should be highlighted and organised throughout the note system to create multiple associations and links between key ideas.

This system for organisation is somewhat similar to the system used to organise topics and keywords from syllabuses.

Revision cards

Although these are very similar to notes generated in the note-taking strategy we just talked about, the key difference between notes and revision cards is that the cards are a much more condensed. They are particularly good for memorisation because of this.

Diagrams and charts

Visual learners benefit most from the use of diagrams and charts, at least when it comes to memorisation of facts, ideas and key concepts.

The effectiveness of diagrams and charts, however, can be maximised through the use of multiple colour systems, keyword and concept systems, and systems for organised development of these charts and diagrams.

Creating diagrams and charts and posting them on walls or other surfaces can be very useful for visual learners.

For planning/organising essay responses, diagrams and charts can be very helpful, too. So if your child does (or thinks they might) work effectively with this kind of support, knowing that they are going to have some written responses to produce in their exams, they should practise using diagrams and charts to outline such responses.

You can help your child with this process by helping them work through practice exams and reviewing the planning and organisational elements they develop to help organising their thinking.

Group or paired revision

Sometimes two heads are better than one. Sometimes people learn better when they have one or more people learning and revising with them.

So long as the focus is actually on revision – not socialising or otherwise wasting time – if your child wants to revise with a study group or they think that they might revise more effectively with a partner or group of partners, they should consider using this revision approach. You should also be supportive.

A key advantage, aside from the fact that it suits some learners, is that students can test each other on exam topics and issues. They can also provide constructive criticism and feedback on how well one person is understanding and remembering concepts and facts, not to mention how well they are answering questions that are asked of them.

If your child is taking one or more foreign languages at GCSE (which they probably are), group learning may also be a great idea for preparing for oral and listening exams.

'Sometimes two heads are better than one. Sometimes people learn better when they have one or more people learning and revising with them.'

Summing up

- Your child will undertake both coursework and exams at GCSE for most of the subjects they are studying.

- Different elements of their GCSE syllabus will be assessed, either under test conditions or on the basis of coursework.

- In most cases, your child will not have the option to choose between taking an exam or producing coursework. However, if they are given a choice, it is important that they consider their overall strengths in testing scenarios – whether they tend to perform better under exam conditions or with more time and resources to exercise creativity.

- Reviewing mock scores as they are available to you will help in the overall preparation for GCSE exams, especially in the prioritisation of goals and management of time for revision.

- Study leave is an important part of preparing, not only for GCSE exams but also for higher education and eventually a career.

- Since this is the first time that your child has experienced 'study leave' – taking responsibility for their learning – they need to take some time to figure out what study leave entails and what is going to work best for them.

- The key to making study leave successful, however, is time management.

- Study leave is not a break from work or an opportunity to do other things (work, hang out with friends, do nothing, for example).

- Responsible work and revision habits are important and you should help your child to make them a priority both prior to and during study leave.

- Your child needs to find a revision strategy that works for them, keeping in mind that everyone learns differently and different subjects may be better studied in a particular way (e.g. foreign language study might benefit from group study).

- As a parent, you can support your child in their revision by helping them realise what strategies might work best for them, applying your own knowledge of their abilities and skills.

Need2Know

Chapter Six

Before Exam Day

Establishing exam day schedules

Assuming your child revises and manages their time relatively well (incorporating some of the ideas we have suggested here with your help), at some point during their GCSE revision process, they (and you) are going to need to begin preparing for actual exams.

For several reasons, the most important thing for exam day is what might very well be called an exam day schedule. Not only do you need to make sure that the date, time and location of exams are accurately written down, it helps to have a schedule in place on exam day to minimise stress and help ensure that your child gets to their exam location on time.

To help your child keep track of their exam day schedules, make sure you write down the time, date and location of exams and post the information in several different places – prominently.

It is not uncommon for students (and parents) to misread this crucial information about exams (and other important appointments), especially if the information is being checked at the last minute.

Save your child the stress of missing their exams or going to the wrong location by establishing a couple of reminders both prior to and on the day of the exam.

Organising your child for exam day

Preparation is the father of inspiration, so make sure that you do all you can to prepare your child for exam success.

'To help your child keep track of their exam day schedules, make sure you write down the time, date and location of exams and post the information in several different places – prominently.'

Getting the right equipment

The day before your child's first exam (at the very latest) make sure that they have the following ready to take with them as a kind of 'exam kit':

- 2B pencils.
- At least three blue or black ink, biro or reliable roller ball pens, or ink cartridge pens.
- If they have ink or roller ball pens, have back-up pens (at least two) and back-up refills for the ink.
- Two erasers.
- A ruler.
- Any special equipment – e.g. maths, science and general studies exams may require a calculator, a compass; certain exams may also require your child to take texts (books) that they have been studying.

To keep this equipment together, offer either a plastic bag, a couple of elastic bands, or a clear pencil case.

Clothing and shoes also constitute equipment for exams – your child should be wearing comfortable clothes and shoes.

Layers may be a good idea, allowing that exam rooms can sometimes be very cold or very warm and the weather outside may be totally different.

Getting a good night's sleep

It is going to be important that your child is able to focus for a considerable length of time on exam day. To give them the best chance of managing this, it is important that they get a good amount of sleep prior to exam day.

Help them to avoid late night revision, television time, or staying out late. All of these sorts of things can be unduly tiring.

For the body to feel rested, it must have the opportunity to go through a normal sleep cycle – that means as little interruption as possible.

Make sure that your child goes to bed and to sleep early the nights before exams. Give them a gentle reminder if they need it.

Ideally, they should get somewhere between 7 and 9 hours sleep on the night before their exams to be able to focus properly.

It may also be a good idea for them to set their alarm about a half an hour to an hour before they usually get up so that they are literally giving themselves a head start. You may want to do the same. This way at the very least, your child will have more time to wake up on exam day, to take a shower and eat a proper breakfast. Having time to go through these routines will help them stay calm, and them being calm (or at least calmer) should help you. The more they have to rush, the more aware they are likely to become of what they have in front of them. The more aware they are, the more likely they are to start feeling overwhelmed or panicked.

It might even be that they start thinking about what they have been revising in preparation for their exam, which is something you want to discourage. This is not the best idea on the morning before an exam. You should encourage your child to try to be clear-headed, calm and relaxed. Help them to trust in the fact that their focus will kick in when they are sitting down at their desk, not before.

Minimising the need to rush out the door also helps to minimise exam stress and maximise efficiency on the day.

'On exam day, like every other day, the most important meal is definitely breakfast.'

Make sure they are eating properly

There's a lot of information out there about the benefits of a balanced diet for the maintenance of concentration and energy levels. For GCSE success, it is important that your child is eating properly, especially on exam day.

On exam day, like every other day, the most important meal is definitely breakfast. This is the meal that jump-starts the body, boosting energy levels but boosting them appropriately, so long as your child makes healthy choices about food.

One of the reasons your child should set their alarm half an hour early, is so they can take the time and enjoy a hearty breakfast.

Protein is the essential element for an exam-day breakfast. The benefit of protein is that it provides a fairly steady release of energy.

A breakfast of eggs, cheese, or other high-protein foods is a good idea versus high-sugar cereals.

The disadvantage of high-sugar foods, especially for breakfast, is that they provide a sudden burst of energy followed by an inevitable crash.

Having a steady energy level is going to be important for your child to sustain their focus throughout their exam day.

In addition to a high-protein breakfast, though, it does make sense to give your child a couple of healthy snacks to have on hand. Rather than chocolate bars or junk food, give your child a plastic bag of healthy snacks such as bananas, apples, granola bars or nuts.

A supply of bottled water is also a good idea on exam day and something you can easily organise for your child. Prepare a snack bag for your child the night before their exam day and leave a reminder for them to pick it up before leaving.

Helping your child to slow down

Making sure your child is prepared will help to avoid them going anywhere or doing anything in too much of a hurry. Especially on exam day, it is a really bad idea to rush.

If your child is rushing about in the early morning before an exam, it is going to be difficult for them to refocus on their exam once they are sitting down and being told to get started on their work.

Obviously you want your child to be able to focus on their exam right away, but everyone needs some time to adjust. Do what you can to give them the time to be methodical and organised. Help them to slow down and think about what they are doing at every stage.

Another problem with rushing is that it tends to leave people less than level-headed. It is not unknown for there to be issues with getting from A to B, especially when in a rush.

If your child is in a rush and finding that things are not absolutely going their way on exam day, even before they have sat down for their examination, they are likely to have issues with even the most practical of steps, such as finding an alternate route to get to school on time if there is a problem.

Prior to exam day, it is going to be useful to help your child identify one or two techniques for slowing down and calming down if they are beginning to feel overwhelmed.

Last-minute revision tips

Don't overload on the last-minute revision – emphasise this to your child as a final pointer for preparing for exams.

In theory, it should only be necessary for your child to do a final check of key facts and pointers if they have actually done their revisions. Of course, they may not feel that they have done as much revision as they could have. It's often very typical for students to panic, thinking that they haven't covered everything. Chances are, though, that they are not the most objective when it comes to assessing this issue. In fact, hours, minutes before their exam, your child is very likely going to experience self-doubt and worry about what they have been studying – have they done a good job remembering everything they need to?

In all likelihood, they will think 'no', but you need to encourage them to tell themselves 'yes'. Because you will have had the opportunity to watch them work, to oversee their revision, you will fairly objectively be able to determine how much revision they have done. Even you should insist that 'yes', they have done enough revision, whether you happen to believe it or not. The last thing your child needs on exam day is to be feeling doubt and uncertainty because they have not revised enough.

Encourage your child *not* to let negative feelings cloud their judgement at the last minute. Even if they have not managed to effectively prepare for their exams, it is only going to increase their stress levels to try and learn new information when they have just hours or even minutes to spare. It will amount to an ineffective use of time. It is far better, if actually your child is unprepared, for them to concentrate on remaining calm and focused; keeping things in perspective.

'Don't overload on the last-minute revision – emphasise this to your child as a final pointer for preparing for exams.'

If your child has prepared effectively, then they will perform better if they manage to stay calm.

If your child really hasn't prepared for their exams, though, you should still avoid being too critical. You should also encourage them to avoid being too critical.

Remind your child: even if they don't get the results they want at GCSE, these exams are a means to an end and there are always different ways to achieve their goals.

Summing Up

- Your main goal on exam day is to minimise your child's stress levels, and your own.

- Make sure you and your child know the time, date and location of the exam – double-check this information for accuracy before exam day but also check on exam day.

- Encourage your child to eat a healthy breakfast and pack a collection of healthy snacks plus water to keep their energy up during their exams.

- Encourage your child to try a couple of relaxation techniques to focus and stay calm right before their exam experience begins.

- Minimise last-minute disasters by having back-up plans in place if, for instance, your child misses a bus or leaves their pens and pencils at home. Encourage your child to be prepared for exam day issues in order to avoid disasters.

- It is extremely important that your child avoids last-minute revision. Encourage them to repeat this as a mantra to themselves.

Chapter Seven

Coping Through the Exam Period

Take it one day at a time

Perhaps the hardest thing about the exam period is dealing with the ups and downs of stress levels. You will probably find yourself close to being at your peak for stress and anxiety as you watch your child go through their own stresses.

How do you survive? How does your child survive?

The simple answer – take it a day at a time.

Give yourself and your child plenty of opportunities to relax, and try to keep the lines of communication open. Communication is key to minimising stress and conflict in just about any setting. It minimises stress that can be the result of simple misunderstanding or misjudgement.

Try to be open-minded and understanding about what your child is going through. After all, it is very common for GCSE students to be anxious and stressed out about revision and about individual exams, even if they are very well prepared and very capable of performing well.

Help your child to reduce their stress levels

On the other hand, it is of course extremely unhelpful if your child is getting so anxious that they are spending more time worrying about their exams than actually revising or preparing for exams.

'Give yourself and your child plenty of opportunities to relax, and try to keep the lines of communication open.'

Learning a couple of relaxation techniques and incorporating them into your day may be a good idea to help you relax. It is an even better idea for your child, though, and it is definitely worth considering ways that you can actually plan to use relaxation techniques together.

Thinking positive is another phenomenally simple but effective strategy for relaxing and improving your mood.

How do you 'think positive'? Challenge yourself and your child to avoid using negative words or making negative statements such as 'I can't' or 'I don't know'.

'Your goal, as a parent, is to be understanding and supportive during your child's study leave and during their exams. The best way to do this is to talk to your child.'

Talk it through

Your goal, as a parent, is to be understanding and supportive during your child's study leave and during their exams. The best way to do this is to talk to your child.

For one thing, evidence shows that simply talking about stressful situations can go a long way to reducing stress. Consider setting aside a regular time to talk to your child about what they are worrying about.

Helping your child to enjoy the night off

Another strategy that may very well go hand in hand with simply talking, is taking some time to relax. Set aside an evening and encourage your child to take the time to read a book or watch a movie, go for a walk in the park or perhaps go out for a quiet evening. You can easily transform it into a family night or a special night for you and your parents.

This strategy works simply because GCSE students can feel that their work is becoming monotonous or their revision is becoming ineffective. When your child is stuck staring at their books and other revision materials for extended periods, they are bound to feel bored or overwhelmed at some point, even if it is only for a short period. Giving them a break, a way to switch the pace of the study leave or exam period, is a great way to not only reinforce your relationship through this time, but also helps them relax and summon the energy to refocus.

Developing a strategy for answering questions

There are a number of strategies for answering questions.

GCSE exams may very well be the first time your child has had to really think about what constitutes an effective exam strategy. If your child has a workable strategy, though, and one that they have practised as part of their revision, it will help them feel more in control as exams approach.

Among the most effective strategies are:

- Answering all the questions, even if they don't know the answer – This is a strategy that works for multiple choice tests, your child may also apply this strategy if they think they have at least a vague idea of what the answer to a question might be.

- Answering questions with the most marks first – If your child struggles to get through exams answering all the questions, then learning to identify the question with the most available marks and beginning with it may be a good way for your child to maximise their potential for exam success.

If they miss out only those questions that have a small number of marks available, it is at least possible to achieve a high score if they have answered the most valuable questions first.

There are also a number of general tips that they can review to compile their exam-taking strategy:

- Avoid spending too long on any one question (also known as pacing) – Help your child to realise that if they get stuck on a single question or a series of questions in their exam, spending too much time on those questions in proportion to the number of questions in the exam (the marks available and the time allowed), they risk a poor grade based on a simple mistake.

  Spending too much time on a single question leaves insufficient time to answer the remaining questions, costing a lot of marks.

  Pacing is something you can help your child to work on, though, when they are working on practice exams. You can oversee your child's practice exam efforts and help your child to keep track of how they are answering questions.

- Allow time to double-check answers – Being thorough is often particularly difficult under exam pressure. However, if you can help your child to get into the habit of double-checking, even triple-checking, their answers to questions, you will be helping them to avoid careless mistakes.

- Tackle difficult questions last – This is a technique that has to be practised, but your child should try to get into the habit of leaving difficult questions until last in their examinations. If they use this technique appropriately, they will always be able to come back to the more difficult question or questions later.

Another tip to offer to your child and encourage them to incorporate as an exam strategy:

- Read (and then re-read) the instructions – This is something that your child's teachers will most likely repeat several times over. Careless mistakes are going to be one of the biggest problems going through GCSE exams. Why? Because everyone makes mistakes under pressure, especially when they are anxious. The more you can do to help your child learn to avoid these types of mistakes, the more you and your child can stay relaxed through the exam period. If your child becomes disciplined about this, you can at least be sure that they are scoring maximum points where they can.

Beyond these tips and strategies, though, encourage your child to make reading the question several times something they do every time they sit down to take an exam. Your child should also make a habit of reviewing the front page of their answer booklet and any other sources of exam instructions for clarification on instructions.

If your child can remember to double-check this information, they will certainly improve their chances of success at GCSE by cutting down on the risk of careless mistakes when answering questions during exams.

Forget about each exam once it is over

This is another one of those pieces of advice that just about everyone offers to students facing GCSE exams. Still, if your child can actually follow it, they will almost certainly set themselves on the path to success in the end.

A major problem with exam stress is that it can build as the exam period continues. If you can teach your child to detach themselves from each individual exam once it is complete, you can help them increase their chances of exam success overall.

Everyone tends to feel different after their exams. Many wish they had had more time. Many others openly worry about the answers they gave to specific questions in the exam.

To help your child save a lot of worry, encourage them to avoid discussing their answers or these kinds of concerns with their fellow students. After all, there is no advantage. Your child can't go back in time, even just to check that they remember the details of a question accurately.

The best thing your child can do, once an exam is done, is forget about it. Have them go and do something to help themselves relax, replenish, and hit the ground running with the revision they have left do.

When your child is finished with all of their exams, though, you might want to encourage them to take a day or two to really reward themselves.

Plan for post-16

It is very likely that you and your child will at least start to do some post-16/post-GCSE planning before your child's final GCSE exam. In fact, you should probably encourage your child to start thinking about post-GCSE options before the beginning of Year 11.

The advantage of planning ahead is that by the time your child has their exams out of the way, they can do some important exploration of career interests, applying for work experience positions, for instance, or simply examining A level or even university options. Planning ahead gives you and your child time to be flexible if things don't work out exactly as planned.

The most obvious thing to look at is your child's post-GCSE options. Planning A level choices is something that becomes relatively time-sensitive as GCSE exams are finished.

'If you can teach your child to detach themselves from each individual exam once it is complete, you can help them increase their chances of exam success overall.'

Because the vast majority of people today stay on to complete A levels and go to some form of higher education institution, chances are that your child is also going to pursue A levels after GCSE.

Even if it is not the easiest option for your child (something you should discuss with them and their teachers) or their preferred option, having A levels and even some form of degree is going to give them more flexibility in the future, whatever it is that they want to do initially.

The summer before Year 11 is a really good time for your child to put in some of the leg work to figure out what their post-16 choices are going to be and, most likely, what their A level selections are going to be.

Helping your child to think about A level options

Your child will have to start to get an idea of what A level subjects they want to study before the end of Year 11. Obviously, this takes some planning. It is important for your child to put some serious thought into their subject choices, as with GCSE options.

Unlike GCSEs, though, when your child is studying for A levels, they are really preparing for university entrance or even a career. It is important that their A level options, more so than GCSE, give some indication of their intentions or at least of their interests for careers.

Organising work experience for your child

Colleges and employers are always impressed when you can demonstrate your interest in a given subject or career. One of the best ways to do this by the time you are working on or even done with your GCSEs is by having a couple of work experience placements under your belt.

As a post-16 activity, sit down with your child and have them make a list of the careers or jobs they are interested in or just the degree subjects they are considering.

Work out a list of relevant jobs that your child might like to 'try out' by way of work experience.

'Planning ahead gives you and your child time to be flexible if things don't work out exactly as planned.'

Need2Know

Go to the careers advisor at your child's school to see what opions might be available for work experience.

Once your child has a list of jobs that interest them, check out some local businesses or talk to the careers advisor about prospective work experience placements that they might recommend based on your child's interests.

See if your child can get a position for the summer to get some useful experience and a bit of a distraction from results day.

Encouraging your child to be active

You can do a lot to support your child after their GCSE exams, before results day, simply by encouraging them to be active and productive. They might consider a summer job, a working holiday, even a regular holiday that will allow them to develop skills or learn something new at the same time that they are being given the opportunity to relax and rejuvenate after exams.

Summing Up

- Give your child plenty of opportunity to relax and de-stress through the exam period.

- Encourage your child to develop a couple of basic relaxation techniques to help themselves maintain focused and reduce anxiety.

- Encourage your child to communicate about any problems that they are experiencing. Not only will talking help your child to keep the lines of communication open, it may very well help them cure their anxiety all together.

- Encourage your child to motivate themselves through the exam period by planning ahead and considering post-GCSE options such as A levels.

Chapter Eight

Coping With Results Day and Moving On From GCSEs

Keeping things in perspective

Results day tends to creep up on you. Hopefully, though, you and your child have prepared for this day. You should have targets – the ideal outcomes – which were the goals for study, revision, and exam periods. You should also have discussed back-up options with your child (the 'what ifs' of not getting the results that they want).

You should also have had an opportunity to sit down with your child and their teachers, perhaps even their careers advisor, for a collaborative discussion on the options open to them.

Even with a plan in place, though, don't be surprised if your child is anxious about results day.

They will need to decide, among other things, whether they want you to go with them to get the results. Most students (in fact, almost all) want their parents on hand. But if your child feels they want to go alone or if you are unable to attend for whatever reason, rest assured that everyone will get through the experience.

Distraction will help pass the time

In the days and weeks leading up to results day, think about planning some distractions for yourself and your child.

Encourage your child to use this time for community service projects, extracurricular activities, career training, work experience or paid employment, or some combination of these.

The day before results day, however, have some quality time for rest and relaxation.

Set this day aside, regardless of what else you are doing and regardless of whatever your child has been doing over the holidays.

A nice meal or a movie night will provide the right kind of distraction the night before results day.

It sounds obvious, but it is important for your child to get a good night's sleep before results day too. In many respects, results day should be treated as a kind of exam day. Exhaustion in any degree – even if it's just one bad night's sleep – is not going to help the stress of results day. A good night's sleep and a sense of relaxation will also promote a level head.

Going prepared on the day

You need to make sure that you and your child have the right time, date and location information for results day.

Put the details on a calendar, set up reminders for you and your child, just as with exams.

Just as with exam day appointments, your child will need to have back ups for getting to the appointed place at the appointed time. Even if you are planning on going with them to pick up their results, make sure that you have a back-up plan – another way for you to get there, someone else to go with them – in case you are detained for any reason.

Having a back-up plan

Perhaps the smartest thing your child can do for themselves on results day is go in there with a clear plan to handle most if not all of the day's possible outcomes.

What do we mean by this?

Simple. Make sure they know their options. Write them down if necessary. In fact, it might be easier if they do write them down.

Suggest using the following general template:

'If W happens I can do X Y, or Z.'

Having a back-up plan will help you and your child keep things in perspective. Remember, even at GCSE, nothing is set in stone about your child's future.

If they don't achieve the grades they want, instead of panicking, having options will help them feel empowered, at least by the time the dust has settled.

Encourage your child to talk to their teachers about their possible options for retaking exams or redoing coursework if that seems like something that might benefit.

Ask the school about the possibility of repeating a year if that might be something that would help.

In fact, encourage your child to ask questions (or ask them yourself) before results day so you have the answers to work with.

Reward your child whatever the outcome

Whatever happens on results day, set aside time to celebrate what your child has achieved over the two years of GCSE study.

Give your child a break and a reward. Whether it is a meal out with family, a night out with friends, or a quiet evening to just relax, let them know that you are proud of all the work that they have done and what they have achieved, whatever that may be.

'Perhaps the smartest thing your child can do for themselves on results day is go in there with a clear plan to handle most if not all of the day's possible outcomes.'

Acknowledging the end of their GCSE experience, marked by results day, will give them a sense of closure and help them prepare to move on to the next stage.

What next? Know your child's post-16 options

After results day, there are decisions to be made. Those decisions may not seem like the biggest decisions that have to be made for your child's education, but in some cases, they are.

Your child has the option to leave school at sixteen. A level studies do not have to be pursued at their current school. They have options not only as to where they study for A levels but whether they study A levels at all. They could consider studying for an International Baccalaureate (IB) or another qualification that could set them on the road to a successful career. It is important to acknowledge that A level examinations, and even university, are not right for everyone.

Talk to your child's teachers and the careers advisor at their school. You should also make an appointment to meet with the person who oversees the sixth form at your child's school to discuss the benefits and the options for them to stay on for A level.

If your child has not achieved the grades they want at GCSE, they always have the option to retake GCSE exams, staying back for one or even two years to redo their GCSEs. If you think this may be a viable option for your child, it is important that you talk to them about this and what it would entail. You should also discuss the situation with teachers and other support and administrative staff at your child's school.

'Whatever happens on results day, set aside time to celebrate what your child has achieved over the two years of GCSE study.'

Helping your child to make the right decision

With your child's GCSE results on hand, you can help them make a decision about what they want to do next. You can review options and see the potential for them to excel in different areas.

Of course, it can be difficult as a parent to give your child the freedom of choice, of making their own decisions. This is an important step at the end of GCSE, though, because so much of A level success is going to be determined by how much your child is interested in and motivated by the work they are doing. There is little advantage to forcing your child either to continue on through A level or to stay in an environment that they perhaps no longer feel is right for them.

Encourage your child to think about their long-term future. Talk about your own experiences. Encourage them to talk to other friends and relatives about the future, about their plans and interests.

You should also explain to your child that going on into higher education is often the smart move long term because of the way that the job market is structured today, and A levels are a very different experience from GCSE for most students.

Discuss what your child would like to do. Listen to their ideas. Perhaps they want to take a gap year. Perhaps they want to study A levels but at a different school. Perhaps they want to stay where they are and continue to sixth form.

Talk about the options and weigh up the pros and cons to help your child in their decision. You should also encourage them to think about developing a relatively long-term plan for themselves and an idea about where they want to be in the future – what they want to do for a career.

> 'Discuss what your child would like to do. Listen to their ideas.'

Considering options for sixth form and A level

Assuming your child does consider A level, you will have to decide with them which is the best school and what are the best subject options for them. What subjects should they study at A level? What do they want to study? Where do they want to complete their A level studies?

If your child intends to remain at their current school, the only decision they need to make is what subjects to study at AS and then at A2. Talking to teachers is the best way to approach this decision-making effort. Looking ahead to possible degree options and career choices will also help.

If your child is interested in considering other schools, or other sixth forms, then this is something you will have to review with them. Make a shortlist of schools that are in your area and offering A level courses.

Try to visit each location and assess the pros and cons of each environment with your child. Talk to subject teachers at each location and find out about the syllabus used for each of the courses your child is considering.

The key is to identify an environment that supports your child's academic needs post-GCSE. Since A levels should involve a lot of independent learning, you need to make sure that your child has the right motivation, supported by access to the right resources. Subject choices are also going to be important. If your child's current school does not offer the A level course they want, look around to see where their preferred subjects may be available.

Supporting your child through the next stages of their education

Whatever your child decides to do post-GCSE, it might feel like a difficult experience to put behind you all. After all, GCSEs are a sizeable milestone for your child. They take up two years of their life and yours. They also lead to a definite conclusion – results – which may or may not be exactly what you and they have hoped for.

The key to helping yourself and your child move past GCSEs is to recognise that they are just another piece in the puzzle. They are to be taken in the context of your child's education, their abilities, interests and goals.

By supporting your child in their post-GCSE decisions and helping them to access resources to make an informed decision, you empower them to take control of their future in a productive and effective way.

'By supporting your child in their post-GCSE decisions and helping them to access resources to make an informed decision, you empower them to take control of their future in a productive and effective way.'

Summing Up

- Results day is scary for just about everyone, but it is important to stay calm and give yourself and your child a break.

- Make sure your child gets a good night's sleep and eats a healthy breakfast on results day.

- Make sure you double-check and write down the date, time and location for your child's results day.

- Have a back-up plan to get your child through results day.

- Ask your child to determine whether they want you – one or both parents – to go along (most students do). Ask them to think about what support they want, if any, from family or friends, and respect their decision.

- Talk to your child to prepare solutions for all foreseeable outcomes.

- Reward your child and celebrate their achievements over the last two years whatever the outcome on results day.

- Celebrate what your child has achieved with their GCSEs.

- Help them prepare for the next step by giving them the opportunity to acknowledge what they have completed over the two years of GCSE study.

- The next step for most people is A levels, but encourage your child to consider their options and make an informed decision.

- Consider the pros and cons of a gap year, sixth form, the workforce, or pursuit of other qualifications.

Help List

GCSE Resources

National Academic Recognition IC, Ecctis

Oriel House, Oriel Road, Cheltenham, SL50 1XP
Tel: 0871 330 7033
www.naric.org.uk
This is the national agency based in the UK that is officially responsible for providing information, advice and expert opinion on vocational, academic and professional skills and qualifications from over 180 countries worldwide.

OCR Coventry Office

Progress House, Westwood Way, Coventry, CV4 8JQ
Tel: 02476 851509
vocational.qualifications@ocr.org.uk

OCR Cymru

Windsor House, Windsor Lane, Caerdydd/Cardiff, Wales, CF10 3DE
Email: ocr-cymru@ocr.org.uk
Tel: 02920 537 810
www.ocr.org.uk/cymru
This office provides a range of specialist support services to customers across Wales. These services include advice, quality assurance support and training.

OCR Ireland

Riverwood House, Newforge Lane, Belfast, Northern Ireland, BT9 5NW
Tel: 02890 669 797
ocr-ireland@ocr.org.uk
www.ocr.org.uk/ireland/
This office provides a range of specialist support services to customers in both Northern Ireland and the Republic of Ireland. These services include advice, quality assurance support and training.

Oxford, Cambridge and RSA Examinations (OCR)

Tel: 01223 553998
general.qualifications@ocr.org.uk

University of Cambridge International Examinations

(Cambridge, UK Office)
Tel: 01223 553554
This is the Cambridge University exam board contact for the United Kingdom,
Ireland and the Faroe Islands.

Book List

GCSEs - What Can a Parent Do?
By Julie Casey.

How to Help Your Child Succeed at School: The Essential Guide for Every Parent
By Dr. Dominic Wyse.

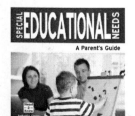  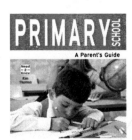 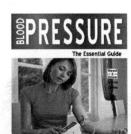